Spirit Blown Wheat

A collection of Prayer Poems and Tidbits

By

Terry L Azeltine, IA

SPIRIT BLOWN WHEAT

A collection of Prayer Poems and Tidbits

ISBN: 978-1-300-10323-3

Dedication

I would like to dedicate this book
to my friends and family. Especially
to my Ignatian Associates Community
and the many Jesuit mentors who have
appeared along my life path.

This is a collection of prayer poems and
tidbits that I have compiled and
published to my blog "Spirit Blown Wheat".
www.spriritblownwheat.blogspot.com

These prayer poems and tidbits were composed
over the course of a year. They are the fruit
of my daily prayer and walk with Jesus.

What Does Jesus Teach?

Some may point to the Beatitudes of the Sermon on the Mount. I look to my life's experience and ask. What have I learned in my faith journey? If I were one of Jesus' Disciples, would He describe me as being "Meek and Humble of Spirit"? "Tired and weary", "Persecuted", "Reviled" etc… etc… Or more specifically, would he bless me as he blessed his Disciples in the Sermon on the Mount.

My faith journey has no way of answering these questions.
Who would know my score on these accounts save the Father, Son and Holy Spirit?

Albert Einstein is credited as saying "Imagination is more important than Knowledge". Can we Christians extrapolate from this to say? "Faith is more important than reason". I can recall of the times when I have taken reason to the extremes and how it has failed me. God's thoughts are not ours and they are certainly much higher than ours. I say if we are to ask for an increase, make it be in Faith. +

Earthen Vessels

So, it is, we Earthen Vessels.
Earthen Vessels for our Soul.
And then we add the
Holy Spirit. That we share in
Life Divine. To us a guide we
do always find. And so we walk beside
our shepherd. Jesus, there for you and I.
Therein, his promise for us to find.
Eternal Life for now and always. +

Sowing the seeds of Prayer

Cultivating the Ground and caring for
what is sown is important.
I am, by praying, both planting and
Caring for the seed of the Word
Not just the seeds of the Word, but also the
Seeds of Faith, Joy, Love etc…
As is said in Holy Scripture, these seeds may
fall
Among the thorns of life and produce nothing.
However, some seeds find
Fertile ground and return a harvest of
Ten or a hundred fold. It is my hope that my
mind is
Fertile ground for the good seed.
I look forward to Harvest time with a Joyful
Heart. +

I am forgiven

Giving the gift of forgiveness to others is a gift for the
Giver and the forgiven. To paraphrase Scripture,
"Those whose sins you forgive are forgiven".
What a freeing gift to one's self.
Jesus freely gave this gift to all.
"Peter approached Jesus and asked him,
Lord, if my brother sins against me,
how often must I forgive him?"
Jesus answered, "I say to you, not seven times but seventy-seven times."
(Mt 18:21). I choose to think of forgiveness as nourishment for
our relationships. To quote a friend:
"What we love is essential". +

New Day

A little of this, a little of that.
Often times, when praying, there
seems to be just a lot of clutter and
disconnected “stuff”. Where to start
is the challenge. It seems that when I start
by Offering the Lord my day, it all goes well.
This, mixed with faith and hope throughout
the day gives me the realization that I am
exactly where the Lord intends me to be.
Knowing that you are following the Lord
Is a great consolation. Each day is
a new blessed day. Jesus I trust you. +

Quiet Please

Who do you listen to? Is it your wife or
husband?
A news program? A television Show? Your
Favorite music? How about Silence? I often
Forget how golden Silence can be. It seems
odd that much can be heard in the silence
of our heart. I consider this a deep treasure and
Resource. Go there, to the Silence of your heart
To just "be". This too can be prayer.+

I found it

Nothing is ever lost with God.
"For the gifts and call of God are irrevocable."
(Rom.11:19)
Praying on this is a real eye opener.
The parable of the lost sheep tells us of the Good Shepard. Can it be that the lamb is never actually lost, but just a little out of sight?
Scripture tells us we can never be separated from
God. See (Rom 8:35, 37-39).
If, in your prayer, Jesus knocks on the door of Your heart, do open the door. And so, where He is, you too may be. And so, nothing of you may ever be lost. +

A Light Within

"

David assembled all Israeli Jerusalem to bring the ark
of the Lord to the place which he had prepared for it."
(1Chr 15:3). In the Old Testament, the ark is the tabernacle Where the Lord dwells. In baptism we are sealed with the Holy Spirit. And so, we become a new Ark. Many are the Gifts of the Holy Spirit. From the Holy Spirit's gift of Courage springs forth Peace. Without Courage, there is precious little Peace. From the holy spirits gift of understanding springs Forth Wisdom. And so, the gift of the Holy Spirit is the gift that we never quite finish unwrapping. I am reminded of a Lyric: "This little light of mine, I'm going to let it shine". +

Speaking of Angels

Gideon, now aware that it had been the angel of the LORD, Said, “Alas, Lord GOD, that I have seen the angel of the LORD face to face”. (Jgs 6:22) I ask, have I ever had an encounter with an Angel? Have you? My faith leads me to say yes. Scripture mentions Angels. We sometimes speak of our Guardian Angels. How about the question: “Does my Guardian Angel know your Guardian Angel?” And so, Angels are present in my faith life. +

Just in Time

In today's gospel we see that some workers worked an hour and others all day. They all received the same wage. Of course we might Question the fairness or equity of this. As this parable teaches in (Matthew 20), we should accept as just pay what the owner of vineyard says is just. So, if today, we repent of our sins and ask forgiveness just in time, should we be received into eternal glory?
Like those who may have begun early. This seems to be
saying yes. +

Being There

In today's Gospel, (Mt 22:1-14) the Kingdom of Heaven is likened to a King who gave a wedding feast for his son. As the parable says, many are invited to the feast but most are too busy to attend. Heaven being like a feast brings images of good food and good fellowship with friends.

I Ask, am I too busy to attend the feast? If so, is Heaven passing me by? Prayer, faith, gratitude and hope are some of the treasures we are graced with in our faith life. These can be ways of saying yes to the King's invitation.

Heaven is eternal. And so, are we too without time for the King's feast? Let's be there.+

With All my Heart

I will give thanks to you, O LORD, with all my heart. (Psalm 138:1) A grateful heart is a Joyful heart. I recall the popular saying "Count your Blessings". When I start to list all my Blessings, I cannot help but be grateful to the LORD. Dear God, Thank You for all prayers heard and all blessings received. Amen +

Let's Dance

How much more than to be the friend of Jesus?
Does he not lift us up?
Up, above it all.
To Dance in the midst of Chaos.
That reassurance of well being and serenity.
We gladly give this away.
Knowing that we are all better for it.
To us be Jesus' love to all. +

I am

In the beginning was the word and the
Word was God. (Genesis). I am the
way the truth and life. (John).
How does the word come to be man?
The word made flesh. (John).
We share in this through the Holy
Spirit. We live and breathe and have
our very existence in God. (Romans).
Which is, in the beginning, the Word.
That word that was made flesh in Jesus.
Thank you Lord for having made me
and preserving me this day.
Thank you for the gift of your Life giving
Holy Spirit in and through the sacrament
Of our Baptism. +

God Loves

"O God, by your name save me. By your strength defend my cause". Psalm 54:3. The Psalms offer wonderful words to pray or sing. When reading the Psalms, I am sometimes taken by one phrase or even just one word. In this way God speaks. In this way God loves. In this way God hears. +

The Light

"Again, Amen, I say to you, if two of you agree on earth about anything for which they Are to pray, it shall be granted them by my heavenly Father. For where two or three are gathered together in my name, there am I in the midst of them." (Matthew 18:19-20) I ask, can two people gathered in Jesus' name pray for anything that is contrary to Loving others as they love themselves? We know that all things work for the good For those who love God, who are called According to his purpose. (Romans 8:28). then God said: Let there be light, and there was light. God saw that the light was Good. God then separated the light from the darkness. (Genesis 1:3-4). +

Rest

Only in God be at rest, my soul,
For from him comes my hope.
He only is my rock and my salvation,
my stronghold ; I shall not be disturbed.
(Psalm 62:6-7). This Psalm seems to
be saying "Take rest in me". I welcome
such rest, Jesus is my Rock and my Salvation.+
+

Choices

Life is full of choices. Many times the choice we make depends on what or who we believe. Prayer can help us determine the best choice. Knowing that "No man can serve two masters" and asking "Is this of God or Not?" can make a difficult
decision easier. "As for me and my house, we will serve the Lord". +

Promises

God always keeps his promises. In today's Gospel we read: For God so loved the world that he gave his only Son, so that everyone who believes in him might not perish but might have eternal life. For God did not send his Son to condemn the world, but that the world might be saved through him. (John 3:16-17)
Hence, now there is no condemnation for those who
are in Christ Jesus. (Romans 8:1).
This is so easily forgotten in the "busy-ness" of the day,
but oh what joy it brings when brought to mind.
+

God and Science

Scripture speaks of our being knitted in the Womb.
Of God knowing our standing up and sitting down.
The LORD will guard your coming and going both
now and forever. (Psalm 121:8). I think back to my
Embryology Class in College. In the study of Embryology,
at that time, there were several bio-chemical processes
of which there were no clear explanations for several
certain cellular decisions or bio-chemical switches. Are we to Presume upon God and his wonderful creation. No,
I say, we are to know that there is a God, an uncaused
Cause without which we would not have been caused
to be. +

Now Time

Interruptions are important. They tell us that something
or someone needs to be heard or seen. Does someone need our prayer in this moment of now time? Our awareness of this can strengthen and guide us as we journey through another day prepared especially for us by God.

+

Jesus is there

In the cry of a child,
In the tear of a mother,
In the baptism of us all,
In the pain of our wounds,
In the joy of our blessings,
In the words of our prayers,
In the healing of our ills.
Jesus is there.
Jesus is all.
Jesus is Lord. +

Humility

It has been a big gift to me
to realize that sometimes I
am full of myself. "We live and
breathe and have our very existence
in God". (Romans) Can we then
say that God is at the center of our
Being? And so, it is when I empty
myself of all my pre-occupations and
my "busyness" that I make room for
all that God wants me to be. +

Hope

Blessed are they who hope in the Lord. (Psalm 40:5a). I believe in God the maker of all things seen and unseen. To hope is to believe. It is to believe in God. It is to believe in things seen. It is to believe in things unseen. An act of prayer is an act of hope. An act of hope is an act of prayer. In my prayer, God assures me that he hears and loves to be heard.

This is my prayer. This is my hope. +

Patience

I trust in the LORD;
my soul trusts in his word.
My soul waits for the LORD
more than the sentinels wait for the dawn.
(Psalm 130:5-6b)
In this psalm, waiting somehow implies trusting and hoping with excited anticipation.
Often, I need to be reminded to wait on the LORD.
My soul seems to know. And so, I wait on the LORD. +

Always Everywhere

We know that all things work for good for those who love God, who are called according to his purpose, (Romans 8:28). How can this be?
Can we find good in all things? Can we find? God in all things? When I don't understand why things have gone a certain way or why a decision
did not go my way, I sometimes call this scripture to mind. Good can be found in all things.
God can be found in all things. Amen. +

The word

The heavens declare the glory of God,
And the firmament proclaims his handiwork.
Day pours out the Word to day,
and night to night imparts knowledge.
(Psalm 19:2-3). In the beginning was the
Word, and the Word was with God,
and the Word was God. (John 1:1).
Each day a new day, a new creation,
a new blessing woven together with
the Word and as the Word. Thank you
God for today's Day, for today's Word,
for today's Night and for you. +

Heart of Love

Faith, Hope and Love, these three words
we call theological virtues. Is there a divine
recipe for these? We know when we have
Faith, Hope and Love. We know we can share
Faith, Hope and Love. My heart affirms
Faith, Hope and Love and is their home. Each
new
Day awakens new Faith, new Hope and
new Love. Give our Love away and it multiplies.
Nourish our Faith with Hope and Love and it
grows.
Trust our Hope and we are strengthened with
the
good guidance of our Lord. +

Yes

All paths lead to Gratitude.
The small "Thank you Lord"
Whispered to myself.
Realizing that where God leads
is best. "Faith never knows
where it is being led, but it loves
and knows the One who is leading" –
Oswald Chambers. My gratitude,
Today, is to pray and accept with open hands,
Open heart and open mind.
"Simply, Yes". +

Christmas

Come Holy Spirit.
Come Holy Night.
Come Holy Day.
Peace for the Soul.
Peace for the Young.
Peace for the Old.
Christ here for you.
Christ here for me.
Christ here for all. +

Life's Tapestry

As I walk along the paths of life.
I choose Jesus as companion.
Together we look at the tapestry of my life.
A tapestry woven by my life happenings. I
see weathered and worn parts of the tapestry
where it seems I may have lingered longer than
needed. I see brightly colored patches where it
seems I have delighted in some Gift from God.
I see the not so bright patches where I may
have stumbled and fell. Even a scorched
patch where I stood to close to the fire.
Always and ever close is Jesus. Sometimes
Sorrow. Sometimes Joy. Sometimes Peace.
Always God's Love and God's Grace. +

Follow

Jesus whispers, Come follow me.
I will make you fishers of men.
And so they did. Into the World
God sent his son so that we might
Have Life and Life abundant.
That our sins may be forgiven.
Abundant gifts; Faith, Hope, Love,
Joy, Peace and Jesus.
Still he calls us to follow.
Oh how wonderful when we do,
“Jesus I Trust You”. +

Perspective

"For we walk by Faith not by sight"
(2 Corinthian's 5:7).
I think of the birds of the air when
I pray on this Scripture. God gave
Them a certain perspective and they
act according to that perspective.
They all seem to know what they are about.
Faith seems to be like that. It is by taking
the next "Faith Step" that we confirm we
are on solid ground and that we come to
know what we are about.
"Jesus I trust you". +

There's not Enough

When all you have is not enough.
When you step out of boat to walk
Towards JESUS and begin to sink.
Just call to JESUS for help and he
Will be there. When God is for you
Who can be against you. Inch by inch
Life's a cinch. +

Wisdom

"Trust in the LORD with all your heart,
on your own intelligence do not rely".
Proverbs 3:5. Are my decisions coming
from the heart level or the intellect level?
Trusting the Lord, even when we do not
Understand, brings Joy and Wisdom.
After all, the Lord's Perspective is not
Our Perspective. +

Earthen Vessels

So, it is, we Earthen Vessels.
Earthen Vessels for our Soul.
And then we add the
Holy Spirit. That we share in
Life Divine. To us a guide we
do always find. And so we walk beside
our shepherd. Jesus, there for you and I.
Therein, his promise for us to find.
Eternal Life for now and always. +

Night

Night is drawing near.
Through the night we journey.
To see, we hope, another day.
Another day to say thank you Lord.
Another day to finish yesterday's work.
Wake me Lord to preserve me this day as your
Child. Hope, Faith and Charity to increase
At your call. Some fruit to bear for your dear
Kingdom. Amen +

Between Heaven and Here

That step between Heaven and Here.
All the love songs look for someone to
Be in love with. Love is essential. Who
Do you love and who are you loved by? Can
you be in
Love with JESUS? Let your heart be touched
By the love that no one but JESUS can give.
In this way you can know JOY. In this way you
Can know PEACE. In the way you can know
HOPE.
In this way you can be all that GOD meant you
to
Be. +

Jesus my Friend

Jesus My Friend,
Each new day to begin.
Good morning to Jesus.
As this day begins.
As this day continues.
So, where is this Jesus?
Oh yes, this is Jesus.
Your peace I do know.
Your love, free to all.
Each new day to begin.+

Walk his Way

Help one another, walk his way.
Hear one another, walk his way.
Encourage one another, walk his way.
See one another, walk his way.
Be with one another, walk his way.
Pray for one another, walk his way.
Love one another, walk his way.
Rise with one another, walk his way. +

www.ingramcontent.com/pod-product-compliance
Ingram Content Group UK Ltd.
Pitfield, Milton Keynes, MK11 3LW, UK
UKHW020215250726
13967UKWH00001B/14

9 781300 103233